The Early Death of Men

The Early Death of Men

Clint Margrave

The New York Quarterly Foundation, Inc.
New York, New York

NYQ Books™ is an imprint of The New York Quarterly Foundation, Inc.

The New York Quarterly Foundation, Inc.
P. O. Box 2015
Old Chelsea Station
New York, NY 10113

www.nyqbooks.org

Copyright © 2012 by Clint Margrave

All rights reserved. No part of this book may be used or reproduced in any manner whatsoever without written permission of the author except in the case of brief quotations embodied in critical articles and reviews.

First Edition

Set in New Baskerville

Layout and Design by Raymond P. Hammond
Cover Design by Anna Badua
Cover Art: "Flex" © Kaileigh Osarczuk | kaileighosarczuk.artspan.com
Author Photo Courtesy of Faria Raji

Library of Congress Control Number: 2012933647

ISBN: 978-1-935520-60-3

The Early Death of Men

Acknowledgments

Grateful acknowledgment is made to the editors of publications where many of these poems first appeared or are forthcoming: *3AM, Ambit, Bank-Heavy, Beggars and Cheeseburgers, Chiron Review, Common Line, The Nervous Breakdown, The New York Quarterly, Pearl, Rattle, Re)verb, Spillway, Spot Literary Magazine, The Tule Review, Word Riot*, as well as the anthologies, *At the Gate: Arrivals and Departures* by Kings Estate Press, and *Beside the City of Angels: An Anthology of Long Beach Poetry* by World Parade Books.

*In memory of my father,
Tallas D. Margrave,
who left too early.*

Contents

Part One: Bodies

In Our Twenties / *15*
Gentle Reminder / *16*
If Lovers Were Books / *18*
How Valentines Fail / *19*
The Bisous Ban / *20*
Clenched Fists / *22*
The First Time Books Saved My Life / *24*
You Are What You Eat / *25*
The Early Death of Men / *27*
Pessoa Died a Virgin / *28*
Preventative / *29*
Man Freed after 100 Hours Trapped in a Lavatory / *30*
Sakura Fairy / *31*
Sad Women / *33*
4th of July Bride / *34*
America's Mattress / *35*
Two, Too Many? / *36*
Exposed / *38*
Forsaken / *39*
Glitch / *40*
Ron Pippin: *Solar Deer*, 2009 / *42*
Literary Training / *43*
Luke / *44*
Corrective Lenses / *45*
Hearing Loss / *47*
Thirty-Three / *48*
Josep Maria Subirachs: *Saint Peter*, 1992 / *49*
Perishable / *50*

Part Two: Minds

My Father's Brain / 53
The Neck of God: Michelangelo's *Separation of Light from Darkness*, 1508-1512 / 54
The Darkness of Libraries / 55
Room / 56
The Astronaut's Diary / 58
What One Learns about Life from an ATM / 59
Muse / 60
Varnish / 62
Radioactive / 63
Is Anybody Out There? / 64
The Role of Art / 66
Darth Vader Holds Up a New York Bank / 67
The Dimming Effect / 69
Bar'd / 71
Pessoa's Typewriter / 73
A Poem Is Not a Teddy Bear / 74
Danger: Avoid Death / 75
The Worst That Can Happen Is You Die / 76
Internal Revenue / 78
The Second Day of the Year / 80
Any Resemblance to Persons Living or Dead Is Purely Coincidental / 81
God's Wife Edited Out of the Bible / 83
The Famous Atheist / 85
What If We Just Stopped Calling Death *Death*? / 86
Marc Chagall: *The Juggler*, 1943 / 88
Time Line / 89
I Don't Believe in Ghosts / 90
Looking in People's Houses / 91
The Math Mortician / 93

All men live enveloped in whale-lines. All are born with halters round their necks; but it is only when caught in the swift, sudden turn of death, that mortals realize the silent, subtle, ever present perils of life.

—Herman Melville, *Moby Dick*

Part One: Bodies

In Our Twenties

Cigarettes were wonderful.
Drinking meant crazy.
Girls felt glorious.
Parents were distant
and hadn't died or fallen ill yet.
Friends seemed plentiful.
Music couldn't be loud enough.
Living with a lover
was like playing house.
Experience was urgent.
Summers meant travel.
Nights seemed infinite.
Hangovers ended quickly.
Work was provisional
until our talents were discovered.
Marriage was a life sentence.
Divorce, parole.
Success was more inevitable than failing.
Suicide seemed romantic.
The world was in love with us.
We were in love with the world.
We swooned inside its magnificent blue form.
We walked with lightness.
We even strutted.
We thought we were invincible.
We thought we were old.

Gentle Reminder

"It's *my* room too," I tell her,
whenever we're fighting
in the middle of the night
and she wants me to go sleep
on the couch in the living room.
"I pay half the rent!"

"But it's not *your* bed!" she likes to say.

This is true.
(It's not my couch
either, but she's forgotten that.)

Four months ago,
when we moved into our small
apartment together,
we had to make a choice
about which furniture to keep,
and which to get rid of.

"Can't we just put it in storage?"
I had tried to suggest, when I was quickly nominated
to donate *my* bed. "Just in case."

"You don't think it's forever?" she had come back at me with.

The other night, things took
an even more ridiculous turn, when,
having spent my last three days
boiling with a fever, an argument
broke out between us.

"I don't wanna fight," I told her. "I already feel
like I'm on my deathbed."

And after placing a cold washcloth
over my forehead, she lay on her side,
adjusted my pillow,
and with a slight smirk
gently reminded me,

"It's not *your* deathbed."

If Lovers Were Books

They wouldn't argue or disagree
or impose on our space
if we didn't want them to.

Their shelf life would be longer,
and we'd always be sure
when we reached the end.

Who knows?

We might even start over,
because they'd always stay the same.
And if we *did* leave, at least
we'd know it was *us* that changed.

We could lay them on their sides,
press our hands against their spines,
and slip between their tattered covers

that we are always free to close.

How Valentines Fail

Blood only passes through the heart for so long
before those groups of distinct
blue vessels that originate within the arteries
begin to harden.

And the heart, to overcompensate,
unknowingly begins
to destroy itself,
and, in turn, the life it supports.

Some ancient cultures believed that the heart was
the dwelling place for the soul.

Today, it is the place which we connect
with those we have affection for—
where we establish those links that are hard
to break.

Our greatest symbol for romantic love.

And how fitting to think the same vessels
that sustain the heart also betray it,
without warning,
when the organ needs them most,

and how, in those pivotal moments of life,
we often become our own combatants.

The Bisous Ban

> *School children given the French kiss-off over swine flu fears*
> —*Guardian UK*

It began in France.
Nobody expected it to happen,
but one morning when Parisians woke up
it was all over the news:

Kissing had been banned.

After a successful trial-run
in bars and restaurants,
authorities had decided
to extend the ruling.

Mothers were now forbidden
from kissing their children off to school.
Lovers could only press lips
25 feet away from all public buildings.

Cities enacted kiss-free zones,
some going as far as
to outlaw it in places
walls were shared.

For many, it was just a simple courtesy:
Secondhand kissing
infringed on the rights of others.
Why should they have to endure
your bad habits?

Before long the ban had spread.
First, through Europe,
then into some Asian countries,
and eventually to North America.

(It was rumored that in Tokyo
you could do it in designated
spots of the city, but even
a mention in L.A. could
get you blacklisted.)

A few countries refused to follow order,
exercised their right to sovereignty,
appealed to the United Nations,
insisted that kissing in moderation
had never hurt anybody.

But there was enough evidence
to suggest differently,
to suggest that kissing could in fact
be a serious hazard to one's health:

not only had it proven to be addicting,
but when done too heavily
for far too long,
had even been known
to kill.

Clenched Fists

I'm thinking of the way we're born with our fists clenched
and how we die with them open.
So much in life depends on
these two simple gestures.
I'm thinking of our hands
and all the ways we use them.
The way we grasp for things.
The way we run our fingers down each other's backs.
The way we show affection,
give pleasure with them,
bring ourselves and others to the point of orgasm.
The way we pick up a pen
and write things down with them.
The way they shake sometimes.
The way we build bridges,
or slip rings onto the fingers
of those we love.
The way they can be used for terrible things,
like strangling somebody
or slapping someone's face.
The way we hold guns with them, light fires,
fly airplanes into buildings.
The way we can pin somebody down against their will
or hold them back from error.
The way we feed ourselves.
The way we steal with them.
The way we hold them up to protect our faces,
or use them to cover our mouths.
The way we make sound.
The way we snap.
The way we take measurements.
The way we raise them over our heads.
Put gloves on to keep them warm,
or to knock each other out.

The way we can somehow map our destinies across them,
or lift ourselves up,
or cut things down,
or hold on tightly to things.
The way we can let them go.

The First Time Books Saved My Life

You know why kids don't value books these days?
Because they've never been smacked
with my mother's wooden spoon.
She threatened me with it whenever I acted up.

This one time, I really outsmarted her.

I went into my room,
pulled two thin hard covers off my shelf,
and stuffed them in the back of my underpants
just as she was coming after me.

When the spoon finally struck, the books padding my ass
snapped the wood in two pieces,
hurling splinters across the entryway,
shocking us both.

This was the first time books saved my life.

And I learned to value them like a monk
learns to value solitude—
even if they didn't do shit when her hand
slammed across my face shortly afterward.

You Are What You Eat

I always thought it was more important
what came out of your mouth than what went in.
But I guess if you have to blame something
for who you are, it might as well be what you eat.
Of course, you are not that pastrami sandwich
or garden burger you had for lunch yesterday,
anymore than you are what shoes you wear,
what you think at certain times of day,
or what you do for a living.

Still, if I could be what I eat,
and if I could eat what I wanted,
I'd eat nothing but the sentences of Ernest Hemingway,
the sculptures of Rodin,
the self-portraits of Egon Schiele,
the paintings of Munch and Picasso and Modigliani.
I'd eat all of France and Italy and Portugal and Spain.
I'd eat the UK too, and Japan,
and the entire Mediterranean.
I'd eat the Musée d'Orsay,
and the bars of Long Beach,
the grapes of Sonoma,
the music of The Jam.

If I could really be what I eat,
I'd eat peace and solitude, love and compassion,
all the greatest things about our species,
books of poetry, philosophy,
films and novels,
walls with beautiful murals.
I'd make meals out of symphonies,
snack on sonnets,
devour Melville's every page.

I'd also eat the greatest scientific discoveries,
Newton's gravity, Einstein's relativity,
Darwin's *Origin of Species*.
I'd eat string theory like string cheese,
wormholes like they were made of gummy,
nebulas like nectarines.
I'd eat the sun and all the gas giants
rolled up inside the curvature of space.
I'd eat distant worlds and parallel ones too,
and the texts of every religion,
every god and goddess,
every Job and Judas,
gobble them all up,
until I'm fat and full and bloated
and have to vomit them out,

just to find myself again.

The Early Death of Men

> *...there are tremendous reproductive benefits to being a winner and tremendous reproductive penalties for being a loser.*
> —David M. Buss

It is said that the male red deer
grows a large body and antlers
to ensure greater success in mating,
the very same traits that make it
vulnerable to an early death.

Between the ages of 16-28
the human male has a mortality
rate nearly 200 percent higher
than the female, stemming from
his own evolved sexual psychology,
a result of the fierce competition for a mate.

Not unlike the red deer,
the human male who risks the most,
experiences the greatest reproductive outcome,
and is, therefore, most likely to avoid
that lonesome punishment we call

longevity.

Pessoa Died a Virgin

They say the closest relationship
he ever had with a woman
led to a mental collapse that
almost put him in a madhouse.
Whatever the cause, it scared him
so much, he never got involved
with another one. Maybe it was
the pipe she hid because she
thought he smoked too much,
or the way she kept punning
his name in French to mean "nobody."
Certainly it didn't help he made her
pray for one of his heteronyms,
and wrote her a letter that said,
"My life revolves around my
literary work….Everything else
is only of secondary interest."
Or maybe it was those "impossible"
adolescent loves, still engrained
in his memory, with their
"deceitful affection," their "shrewd caresses,"
that continued to aggrieve him,
create "cosmic cataclysms" in his soul,
push him to retreat inside
the imagination, teach him early
on what so many of the trampled
only wish they'd known.

Preventative

The doctor assures me that the blood pressure medicine
I'm taking is just a preventative measure.
"This is the age of prevention," he says.
"Not only will it regulate your pulse,
it'll help prevent any future heart attacks."
I wonder where this guy's been all my life.
All the other things he could've prevented:
Divorces and bad haircuts.
Nights spent in drunk tanks or staring
into the endless bottoms of shot glasses.
Friends who weren't really friends.
Psychotic one-night stands with women
who had scars on their wrists and giggled at my bookshelves.
Measures that might've prevented me
from telling people I loved them when I didn't really mean it,
or telling them I hated them when I did.
Measures that might've prevented me
from phone calls or close calls
or marrying someone I didn't know,
staying with someone I knew too well.
Where was this guy to prescribe me my little dose
to swallow every morning and every night
that might've prevented all those other
attacks of the heart?
And, of course, the benefits outweigh the costs.
But I leave his office feeling cold,
wondering about what can't be prevented
with just a pill.

Man Freed after 100 Hours Trapped in a Lavatory

—Reuters

According to the article,
the 55 year old retired Scottish school teacher
was stoical about the whole event saying,
"At least there was a toilet to use."
But I can't help think about the part the news didn't print,
like why nobody came looking for him.
At 55, no wife, no daughter, no son, no friend, nobody to ask,
"Where's David been for the past four days?
He never did come home from
that lawn bowling club in Aberdeen."

Not even a missing persons report.

And why am I so jealous?
Is it because he somehow managed
to avoid all those other traps?
And what did he think about for one hundred hours?
Did he regret the course of his life or was he pleased with it?
Did he wish he brought a newspaper? A book? A pen?
A cell phone? And how many men try to do this
inside their own bathrooms every morning,
away from the wife, the kids, the neighbors, the job,
the bills, the hopelessness?

He called it captivity.
The article called it 'caught.'
I guess it depends how you look at things.

Personally, I think a more appropriate
headline could've read:

"Man Trapped Again After 100 Hours Freed In a Lavatory."

Sakura Fairy

To the Japanese,
sakura is a metaphor
for the ephemeral nature
of life,

beauty in
the brevity of existence,

and how quickly the tree's
tissue-white petals
go gliding
to the ground
each spring,

artists and poets
have depicted
it for centuries,

in songs,
in paintings,
in patterns
on kimonos,

and at a Kyoto bar,

once,

I met a tiny,
drunken,
middle-aged
woman
who wished
only to be
reincarnated

as a cherry
blossom,

her sole mission
in life
to become
a thing
of beauty,

a *sakura* "fairy"
as she put it,

before
vanishing
out the door.

Sad Women

They come to my door.
I don't know what draws
them to me or me to them,
but we sit together late at night,
smoke cigarettes, drink whiskey,
laugh. This one I know likes to
disguise her sadness in a yellow
cup, she brings with her everywhere,
from which she drinks fear,
self-hatred, suicidal thoughts.
She is my favorite. She is the
saddest of all. We pretend to
like each other, long for things
that can never be, let intimate
moments pass when she allows me
to stroke her hair, run my fingers
down the side of her neck,
caress her sadness. And I don't know
what it is that makes a man open
his door for such sad ones like her.
(My friends say I'm "asking" for it,
that it's all in the choices I make.)
But late at night sometimes,
when we're alone together,
I can feel those painful distances
collapse, as if the degrees of
sadness we share have somehow
formed a bridge between us,
the kind from which nobody jumps.

4th of July Bride

She finds it ironic to be getting
married on Independence Day.
Earlier that morning, she's taken out
the word "forever" from her vows.
At the altar, nobody hears her say, "I do."
She knows why brides wear veils.
The family applauds them, toasts to their happiness.
Friends bring gifts and hugs.

After the reception, some of the guests
come back to the hotel to watch the fireworks.
She goes to bed before they leave,
pulls the blanket over her head.
Nobody seems to notice, not even the groom.
He stays up late drinking with his best man.
Two friends consummate the marriage
for them in the bathroom.

When morning comes, empty bottles crowd
a wilted corsage on the nightstand.
Her husband's passed out next to her,
still dressed in his tuxedo.
All the guests have disappeared.
She thinks of the money
her parents spent.

From underneath the blanket
she pulls out her hand
and stares at the shapely red heart
tattooed on her finger as a wedding band.
She marvels at its permanence.
She marvels at the cost
of having it removed.

America's Mattress

America's mattress is the widest
and hardest of all.
Empire-sized.
Twice its original mass
after years of needing replacement.

Most of us lie at the foot
of America's mattress,
reserve our little square,
cram in beside each other,
limbs hanging over its edges,
while the biggest and fattest,
spread out at the top.

Sometimes,
people get killed
trying to make space
on America's mattress.

The end tag is threaded.
Attempts are made
to have it illegally removed.
The middle is sunken.
The rusted springs
poke into our backs,
make it impossible to stretch
without fear the whole frame
will collapse.

Only the privileged sleep peacefully
on America's mattress.
Most of us fidget,
toss and turn with insomniac fits,
hope for the day
we shift our weight
and finally get some rest,
long enough to dream.

Two, Too Many?

It was a match made in Paris.

Juan Baptista dos Santos had two penises
and Blanche Dumas, two vaginas.
There was simply no question
as to what the two had in common.

Still, according to the article I read,
their relationship was horrid,
despite the perfection of finding
the only other person in the world
who could fulfill the other's
sexual appetite.

Of course, when you think about it,
it isn't any surprise really,
given the demands of a relationship
with half as many genitals.

I wonder if Juan, despite his prowess,
ever felt pressured by the demands of having
to satisfy, not one, but two vaginas?
Was it possible both dicks could go limp at the same time?
Had there been Viagra in the 19th century,
would he have had to take two capsules?
Was there twice as much anxiety to make it last,
and twice as much pleasure in doing so?

And what did it mean for their relationship?
Did one feel twice as rejected when the other wasn't in the mood?
Was there twice as much temptation to cheat on each other?
Were their insecurities twice as magnified,
their fights twice as bad?

Did they do twice as many irritating things
like taking twice as long in the bathroom?

According to the article,
their relationship is unparalleled in the history of humanity,
but little is known
about the way that it ended.

Was it the same as everybody else's
or was there twice as much strife?
Did the one who left first
experience twice as much guilt?
The one that got dumped,
twice as much anguish?

Or did they stay together
twice as long as they should've,
like I always did in all
my past relationships,
and experience twice
as much misery?

Exposed

His last night at the hospital,
my dying father was in no condition
to change himself.

The nurse and I slipped his pants down,
and for the first time,
I saw he wasn't circumcised.

With a Jewish mother
and Jewish grandparents,
I wondered how it happened.

At thirty-three, I was shocked
to learn our differences
weren't only on the inside,

that even the most exposed areas
of our masculinity
had kept no covenant.

Forsaken

Then there was David,
whose dad poured kerosene on him
when he was six years old,
lit him up like a sparkler
in a Buena Park motel,

90% of his body charred,
leaving him hairless,
lips swelled like a mouth
inside a suction cup.

Every Friday, we said hello
on the way to chapel
at Eastside Christian,
before filling the pews
with our other classmates,

where we learned about
Christ's bleeding palms,
and the cosmic custody battle
between God and Abraham,

where we learned about
the meaning of sacrifice,
and all the mysterious ways
that fathers loved their sons.

Glitch

sometimes
I find it strange
just to have
pockets,

to walk down the
street with my
hands in them,

or to have
fingers
that clutch
a knife
as I butter
my dinner roll.

sometimes
I find it strange
just
to occupy space
or drive a car
or blink.

And why doesn't
science love us?

And how can there
be a god that does?

And what exactly
does it mean
to live in a vacuum?

And why do I
ask so many
questions?

And who will
answer them?

Ron Pippin: *Solar Deer*, 2009

Solar deer,
who made thee?
Dost thou know?

Your hooves are bolts,
your veins, wires,
your flesh is obsolete.

Monumental figure.

Is the future made of trash and junk?
Part animal, part emblem,
part mad creator?

It seems my deer,
this evolution
cannot be stopped,

that the machine is slowly
consuming you,
as it is me.

Literary Training

"Are you some kind of death rocker?"
asks the skinhead.

My friend and I are hanging out
behind the AMC movie theater,
when he & his cronies
show up
threatening to kick my ass.

I'm fourteen,
timid,
dyed jet black hair,
black pants,
black t-shirt,
a black leather jacket.

"Because if you are,
I suggest you split," he says,
before he head-butts me,
& the blood comes rushing
down my face,

still naive enough
to think this has something
to do with the way I dress,
not aware yet
there will always be those
who hate you
for what they
don't understand,

& sometimes
it's the deepest scar
that cuts the clearest path,

which in my case,
starts at my nose
but ends
at my mouth.

Luke

With one eye open he scans the world.
His parents find it hard to explain how he got this way.
At six months old, a brain tumor paralyzed the right side of his face.
He's never understood why kids made fun of him.
He doesn't talk when he is younger because he is afraid of others.
He comes home crying from school.
By the age of seven, he's already bitter.
In junior high, they are the cruelest.
Girls won't even look at him.
He considers suicide, but doesn't want to hurt his parents.
At lunch he sits with boys so awkward and rejected
none of them say anything.
They spend the hour picking at their faces.
He sees the world with one eye open
which is exactly how he knows the world sees him.
By the time he graduates high school,
he's given up the prospect of ever finding a girlfriend.
His love life will consist of expensive prostitutes in cheap hotel rooms.
When he goes to sleep, he dreams himself in heaven.
At college, the first day of class, his English teacher
writes "Who are you?" on the board.
He makes the comment that's a difficult question.
He knows all the teacher wants is his name.
The other students laugh.
Some roll their eyes.
The pretty girl sitting next to him won't sit there again.
The teacher smiles, his own two eyes scanning to focus
on the ugly young man looking up at him.
The teacher knows he sees more than the rest of them.
The teacher knows with just one eye
he sees more than all the other eyes combined.

Corrective Lenses

I got my eyes checked yesterday.
Turns out I don't have clear vision anymore.
No surprise really.
I've been showing symptoms
for a long time.

"How bad is it?" I asked the doctor.

"You're farsighted," he told me,
which means I can see things in the distance
but not right in front of me.

Apparently, being farsighted
can also leave you fatigued.
"It can even affect the way
you comprehend things," said the doctor.

Again, no surprise.

"You're straining to overcompensate,"
he said, "because
you can't see."

He told me not to worry.
More people than ever
need corrective lenses.

"Good for job security," he said,
"but a terrible time for vision."

And though it's possible
for some to maintain it
throughout their lives,
doing so is extremely rare.

"For most of us, it just goes," he said,
handing me a prescription,
and trying to reassure me,

I'm not alone.

Hearing Loss

For some, it is age-related.
Others are born with it.
Still, there are those for whom hearing loss
is caused by a sudden traumatic break—

that if damaging enough,
can be permanent;
if damaging enough, can puncture
the receptors that control the level at which we hear things:

the receptors that make words distinguishable,
allow past and present voices to meet,
leave traces in the message centers of our brains,
where time holds a vigil,

where memories plot their exits,
where the living must speak loud enough
so the dead do not
impair us.

Thirty-Three

When Christ was crucified.

The number of innings
in the longest baseball game in history.

A vinyl record.

A hexagram.

The amount of vertebrae in the human spine.

What doctors ask patients to say in some countries
when listening to their lungs.

The lowest temperature water remains liquid.

How much of the Earth's land is desert.

The number of cantos in each part of *The Divine Comedy*.

The percentage of sleep an average person needs each day.

How many years it takes the sun to rise
at the same point on the horizon.

The atomic number of arsenic.

A pantheon of Hindu deities.

My father's age when I am born.

The age I have to bury him.

Josep Maria Subirachs: *Saint Peter*, 1992

The world is a labyrinth, Peter.
There are better places to be
than at the side of the son of man.

Like here, at the Sagrada Familia.
Better in the hands of Subirachs
than an unresponsive god.

Oh Peter, you were only being sensible.
Who wouldn't doubt it?
Faith is for the foolhardy.

A good scientist knows
the necessity of experiment,
that conjecture isn't evidence.

Better to be in stone,
than sacrifice one's life
to the mind's delusions.

Better to see the empty tomb
for what it really is,
yours to fill.

Perishable

The last thing we did was empty out the kitchen.
None of us felt comfortable taking home the food,
but my mom insisted everything had been bought the last time
he had gone grocery shopping, and it was a shame to waste it.
It's true, I took a bottle of sake I had given him
as a gift from Japan two years ago,
which I found unopened on the top shelf of the liquor cabinet,
and which I finished shortly after
returning home to my apartment.
But I also took a brand new jar of pickles
that remains untouched in my refrigerator,
a month and a half after his funeral,
and which, just this morning,
I happened to notice,
while reaching in for a carton of milk,
that with its cold tight lid,
the jar is not set to expire until next January—
eleven months after my father
was given the worst kind of news,
ten months after he would ask my mother to call an ambulance,
and only eight and a half from when his own son
would stand in front of a refrigerator
and painfully observe,
that on his last trip grocery shopping,
a man is more perishable than his food.

Part Two: Minds

My Father's Brain

I'm looking at my father's brain.

My sister and I found it
stuffed in an envelope
in my parents' garage
yesterday.

Only weeks before,
it had been alive,
now it was here,
stacked in this box,
with all the other
stuff we don't know
what to do with.

"That's the frontal lobe," my sister says,
picking it up
and turning it around
to show me.

"Can I keep it?" I say,
lifting it into the sun
for a better glimpse.

"Do whatever you want with it,"
she tells me.
"It's yours."

The Neck of God: Michelangelo's *Separation of Light from Darkness*, 1508-1512

Michelangelo knew what separated light from
darkness when he hid a brainstem in
god's neck on the ceiling
of the Sistine Chapel.

He knew it is the brain
that creates the world for us,
through which all signals travel,
from which all must pass.

He knew what separates light
from dark is our consciousness,
that the brainstem in the neck of god *is* god,
without which we are nothing.

Some scholars believe he wanted
to show the future his understanding of anatomy,
others see it as an artistic commentary
on the age of Copernicus,

a record of the enduring clash
between science and dogma,
a battle in which five hundred years later
we still must defend ourselves,

against the zealots of denial
and superstition.

The Darkness of Libraries

Where the light is scarce,
the darkness is accessible,
and given to us for free.

Room

Whenever I buy a cup of coffee,
I always appreciate how the barista will ask,
"Do you need room?"
And I think, what a better world it'd be
if we all just did this.

You're at work, the stress piled up,
when the boss nudges you,
pops the question,
and off you go home for the week.

Your lover, after spending days with you,
wakes up and at the nod of your head,
without saying anything,
gets dressed and leaves.

You're on the freeway,
about to miss the exit,
when the driver in the next lane
sees your blinker,
gently taps his brakes
and with a flash of his lights,
signals you're clear.

Imagine what could happen
at the borders of
India and Pakistan,
Israel and Palestine,
China and Tibet.

Or the inner borders
of harsh judgment
and bitter regret.

Imagine if the pilgrims
had asked the Indians?
Cortez, the Aztecs?
(Just before he turned around his ships.)

Imagine a suicide bomber
ordering his last mortal cup of java,
at a Jerusalem café,
doomsday device
strapped to his chest,
only to be astonished
by the barista's question
nobody in his terrorist training camp
ever bothered to ask.

It's a basic amnesty
carried far
beyond a coffee cup,

that whether or not
it intends to be, says a lot about the importance
of allowing each other space
to feel and think.

"Yes," I always tell the barista
even though I don't take cream.

Because with room nothing ever spills,
creates a dark black stain,
scorches me.

The Astronaut's Diary

> *Columbia astronaut's diary goes on display.*
> —*AP*

Words burn as they enter the world.

No longer weightless,
they spin out of the mind's orbit,
plunge through the atmosphere.

Words burn as they enter the world,

outlive their author,
get eaten up,
displayed,
stuck together
in tightly crumpled wads,

like the charred pages of Ilan Roman's diary,
found in a Texas field,
months after
the space shuttle Columbia
disintegrated.

Words burn as they enter the world.

Some are lost.
Some stolen.
Some ignited
by the stress of temperature.

What One Learns about Life from an ATM

First, choose a language.

Don't ever give anyone
your secret code.

Always answer "yes" when asked:

Do you wish to continue?

Make deposits only.

Try hard
not to
withdraw.

Muse

There's a woman who cries in our neighborhood.
The first time we realized it, my wife and I were in bed.
"Do you hear that?" she asked.
I followed her into the living room
where we both stared out the window.

"Look," said my wife.
There was the woman, sitting on a curb,
head in her hands,
weeping.

"Should we do something?"
"No," I said. "She probably had a fight with her boyfriend."
It must've been around two in the morning.
"Last call," my wife said. "She's probably just drunk.
Let's go back to bed."

We did and never thought much about it
until this woman started popping up on every corner.
I'd see her by the bank, on the pier,
outside the grocery store.
Soon, it became a point of conversation
between us.

"I saw her again today," I'd tell my wife
when she got home.
"Was she doing the same thing?" she'd ask.
"Exactly."

Now it's gotten even worse.

Like this afternoon, while I was trying to write a poem,
she sat directly beneath my window.
I thought maybe the mailman
or passersby would notice,
but they just kept walking.

She never seems to have anywhere to go.
She never has to work
or do her laundry
or take an important phone call.
Some of my friends have even seen her,
asking when they visit:
"Why's she so sad?"

I shrug it off and tell them
there's a part of me
that doesn't want to know,
though I never bother mentioning
the other part,
that doesn't need to ask.

Varnish

How fast a varnish dries
depends on its environment.
The film-forming substance
begins to harden
upon exposure to air.

Always apply and reapply.

And sometimes
let what lies beneath it
stay exposed,
let sunlight make direct contact,
let everything burn.

Or when the protective seal
finally wears
what's left uncovered
will erode,

break apart,

prove unable to adapt to
the cracks and peels
of that which ages,
and cannot be glossed over.

Radioactive

I distrust those who are always seeking light,
always trying to find the positive side of life,
for they are nothing in the dark.

Their light is artificial,
seeks a false radiance that only
ever illuminates the surface.

Understand they need you
more than you need them,
that at their center is a black hole.

Help them to sustain
the light they are always
trying to absorb,

for they cast more shadows
than they know,
and like all bright lights,

the hotter they glow,
the better it is to keep your distance,
so you won't get burned.

Is Anybody Out There?

It was detected in the late 1970s
and never repeated.
A signal from deep space.
For years, scientists tried to find it again,
pointing their radio telescopes
in the same vicinity,
only to get static.

I've been talking to a lot
of my good friends lately,
mostly guys in their thirties,
who feel desperate,
anxious to meet somebody.

And like the scientists,
who years later
still keep listening for that signal,
they keep repeating
the same experiment,
keep pointing their telescopes
in the same vicinity.

They say that I'm lucky.
That they want what I have.
And it's true, I am.
But for years I wasn't.
Searching the skies
and detecting nothing.

I can't make them any predictions.
I can't even explain the science.
I can only tell them just to keep looking.
The lack of a message doesn't mean
there isn't life in the universe;

it also doesn't mean
they're going to like what they discover.

Suppose a signal does come,
but it's the wrong one,
and brings with it
something more savage,
more brutal than they ever imagined.
Something that sets out to destroy them,
like it did me a few years ago,

when I was almost done in
by a violent and destructive creature,
who taught me long before
I ever met the right person,
that it's not always better to make contact:

sometimes,
it's better
to be alone.

The Role of Art

Art is an introvert.

At parties, it sticks to walls
nobody notices.

When it speaks,
it struggles to be heard.

Like all who tell the truth,
Art has few patrons,

is always offending somebody.

Art is solitary,
rebellious,
abstract.

It is *not* communal.

And when embraced too fully,
has a tendency
to crash things down.

Not wishing to be known,
not wishing to be liked,
not wishing the acclaim of
its more popular cousin,
Cliché,

Art is an outcast,

whose only role
is to protect its value,
by doing everything for its own sake,

and hoping that it matters.

Darth Vader Holds Up a New York Bank

-CNN

With the Death Star in foreclosure,
and the Storm Troopers laid off,
he had begun to doubt his
unwavering faith
that the Force would be with him.

Not even his old pal Jabba
was willing to grant him a loan
to pay his child's support anymore,
citing too high a credit risk
in an unstable galactic economy.

The bank surveillance camera showed
a nervous cyborg dressed in camouflage,
one mechanical hand pointing
a lightsaber at the scared young teller;
but it was the heavy breathing
that had ultimately
tipped off authorities.

And as he fled the scene that morning,
Darth Vader felt a tinge of nostalgia
for the good old days,
when he could warp speed himself
out of anything,
or choke a man unconscious
if he really needed to escape.

He despised the life of the petty criminal,
preferring to smash rebel alliances
and seize their assets,
play all those Jedi mind-tricks

that had once earned him a reputation
as CEO of the dark side,

before the bailouts
and calls for reform came,
when the growth of the Empire
had still seemed inevitable,
a long time ago,
in a galaxy far, far away.

The Dimming Effect

The world is getting darker.

Less and less light
can reach the surface
of the Earth each year,

a result of airborne
pollutants that reflect
and diminish sunshine.

And to the harbingers
of doom, all those
who revel in the end,
who would make humans
the next dinosaurs
if it meant Armageddon,

I await your last flicker.

For I am of the few who believe
your bell is soon tolling.

How I grow tired of the way
your religious absurdities,
your apocalyptic visions of hell,
your hypocrite holy wars
contaminate the minds of men

like the way soot from burning
fossil fuel keeps light
from passing
through the atmosphere—

in science,
this effect is
known as 'global dimming'

and recent studies
suggest

the damage *is* reversible.

Bar'd

I walked into a poem the other night.

It had been a long day
and I happened to see a
sign with a great big beckoning
arrow calling me.

Just one, I promised myself.

A couple other guys
I recognized were standing in front,
chain smoking,
pacing back and forth,
deciding whether to go in.

I didn't hesitate.

I walked straight up to the entrance
where a white bearded bouncer
met me and asked if I had
any identification.

He looked at it for a while
and I thought for sure
he was going to deny me.

"It's slow tonight kid," he said finally,
handing it back. "Don't expect to get lucky."

I thanked him
and went in anyway.

He was right.

No music played,
no flames were alight,
the muses had all been thrown out.

It was not my kind of poem.

Pessoa's Typewriter

All the letter keys
were *I*'s,

all the symbol keys,
question marks.

A Poem Is Not a Teddy Bear

—after Tony Hoagland and for him

Nor is it polite, or pretty, or politically correct.
A poem is not a liberal or a Democrat.
A poem is not a Republican either, or a Libertarian.
A poem is not from a particular region of France
or from the East or West.
A poem is not black or white or Scandinavian.
A poem stereotypes, gets angry, feels contempt,
lies sometimes.
You can't hold it close to your chest
or snuggle up to it.
A poem is not running for president.
It doesn't need your vote or want to be your friend.
A poem is a ferocious animal, drool dripping
down its chin—
not a blanky to take to grandma's house
or a tissue to wipe your nose with.
A poem is not a teddy bear,
but if it were, would come unstitched,
dragged too often in the dirt,
too many nights forgotten in the wet cold,
abandoned, decapitated, dumped off,
or chewed up in games of tug of war.
The kind you keep banished to your closet
once you've grown,
cover up its foul old stench
with elegant perfumes and colognes.
The kind that in the minds of others does not exist,
that has been kept hidden so long
scares the shit out of you
when the light from outside shines in,
and you forget what it is.

Danger: Avoid Death

*Winner of the 11th annual wacky warning label contest.

As a matter of fact,
avoid birth if you can.

Avoid infancy.

Avoid school
and puberty
and the humiliation of sex.

Avoid the fear of not being able to love
and the fear of not being loved back.

Avoid the holidays,
and the hostile days,
and the days of regret.

Avoid surgery.

Avoid airplanes,
and tall buildings
and terrorist plots
to blow them up.

Avoid Afghanistan,

and born-agains,
and wish-they'd-never-beens.

Avoid Republicans,

and the urge to die,
the urge to kill.

The urge to do
what you're told.

The Worst That Can Happen Is You Die

I used to tell this to myself when I was younger,
before I dialed
a girl's number I liked
or had to defend myself
in fights at school.
I'm not sure when it started
or how young I was
or how much I'd even thought
about actual dying,
but the words comforted me,
made me brave,
allowed me to stand up to bullies
and figures of authority,
including my parents or teachers
or first bosses
(when getting fired
was a luxury
for a teenager
who still lived at home).

Now I can't remember
the last time I said them.
Even though, at 36,
life pushes more challenges than ever my way,
and there are different fears and different girls
and different figures of authority.
Maybe it's just that I've learned
there can be worse things than dying,
like long illnesses or long *lonelinesses*,
or hurting somebody.
Or maybe it's just my growing
sense of the end
as I pull up to middle age,
and become increasingly aware

that for those who love life,
there's only one true bully,
and sometimes,
the worst that can happen
really is,
that you die.

Internal Revenue

I got a letter from the Internal Revenue Service
asking to examine me for the years 2006-2008.
Apparently, during this time I didn't pay in enough
which is funny because it was during this time
I feel like I paid the most.
You can always appeal, the letter said.

The whole thing upset my wife,
especially since this was from before we got together
when I was briefly engaged to someone else.
"It's mostly my fault," I told her. "I allowed myself to be misled."
"I hate having to pay for the past," she said. "I think you should appeal."

According to the letter, the examination process
didn't mean I owed anything yet.
It also didn't mean I'd been dishonest.
Only I knew that.
Only I knew that much of what I claimed
during those three years was bullshit,
even assisted by friends and family who assured me
I was doing the right thing.

Still, I decided to fight this,
dipped into some files I'd been ignoring for years.
Every statement, every deduction, every mile traveled.
In all truth, it was embarrassing to have to hold up the past like this.
I've never been very good at it.
But something must have triggered this exam.
"Three years is nothing," I told my wife. "We have our whole lives."
Besides, I said, we can always pay in small increments.
"That's what I don't like," she said. "It's all penalties
from not having paid the first time."

We got everything together, sealed it all up, and sent it off—
none of which the Internal Revenue Service would accept.
But it didn't matter, I thought.
These days, I'm much better prepared:
I make sure the more I pay into something,
the more I get something back,
and suffer no appeals.

The Second Day of the Year

No one ever talks about it.

The parties have ended.
Confetti has been swept up and thrown away.
Headaches have disappeared.

And maybe that's why I've always preferred
the second day of the year.

Because it's ordinary, unassuming.

The streets are quiet.
Stores are open.
There are no parades or football games.

You can walk without feeling lonely.

Nobody wants to quit smoking
or propose,
or make promises they can't keep.

On the second day of the year,
nobody expects anything.

Plans are struck down,
couples go on fighting,
bigger and better resolutions get made.

Any Resemblance to Persons Living or Dead Is Purely Coincidental

I don't like it when my wife writes about other guys.
I don't even care if they're fictional.
I don't like it when she makes them say things in her stories,
makes their legs brush up against hers.
I don't like it when her female characters
fall in love with her male ones.

I don't like it when she writes about ex-boyfriends
or ex-lovers or crushes she once had.
I don't like that she even thinks of them to write anything at all.
I don't like how she thinks if she changes their names I won't notice.
I don't like how she stole the argument that it's just "fiction"
from me in the first place and now *I* have to be the hypocrite.
I don't like how she actually calls me that.

The only thing I don't like more is when she writes about me.
I never knew I'd feel this way living with another writer.
I never knew after years of doing it to other people
I wouldn't like it when someone does it to me.
Like what gives her the right?

As you can imagine, my wife doesn't like this at all.
She gets really angry at me.
Calls me a son of bitch (even though she loves my mom).
Says that I'm a worthless phony.
Then she'll storm off into the bedroom
and slam the door.

I'll sit in the living room wondering
what she's doing in there,
just to find her lying across the bed, you guessed it,
writing about me.
I don't like this.

I don't like that there's no way to win this situation.
I don't like that if I get mad at her for writing about me,
she goes into the bedroom and writes about me.
I don't like this at all.

In retaliation, sometimes, I'll go to my desk and write about her too—
like I'm doing right now. Except she's not home.
She's at work revising a story about some other guy
that she just asked me to edit.
I don't like that she thinks it's okay to have me edit
stories about other guys.
This, of course, leads to an argument in which she texts me
the following:

Liar. Hypocrite. You think it's all about you.
You're off my list. Fuck You.

The maddest she ever got was when
I called her ignorant after getting jealous over a story
I'd written about a girl I knew long before her.
I tried to explain I just make shit up sometimes
and it had no bearing on reality—
which was a lie, of course, and completely hypocritical.

But *whatever*.
That's what my last text message just said.
My wife hasn't replied yet.
She's too busy revising the story about that other guy
and now I'm too busy writing about her.
I guess that's the way it goes when two writers live in the same apartment.
I hope someday we'll quit this nonsense
and get back to writing about the stuff that really matters,
like ourselves.

God's Wife Edited Out of the Bible

—Discovery News

It hadn't always been like this,
but as of lately, things had changed.
And the strain of not only running a universe,
but trying to keep a marriage fresh
proved too much for any deity.

For a while, it had been convenient
having someone else around
to divide up all the responsibilities,
like answering prayers,
making sure the right side won its wars,
monitoring people's sex lives.

But there were some miracles
that even God couldn't perform.
And despite His willingness
to seek couples' counseling,
He just couldn't fake it anymore.

After all, there had been no "till death
do us part" in Their wedding vows.
And divorce was simply out of the question.
She'd never relinquish Her share of the Creation,
not to mention the cost of paying
alimony for all eternity.

So, He had Her cut out.
Wiped clean every parable,
every psalm, every covenant,
every birthday card or love letter
She'd ever sent to Him.

Except, despite His best efforts,
traces of her still remained,
surfacing on the fragile stones
of ancient tablets,
in amulets and figurines,
inscribed on pottery.

And God felt sad, realizing He had fucked up.
But by then it was too late.
He found Himself all alone in the universe,
wondering how things got this way,
just like the rest of us.

The Famous Atheist

had come to town to debate the afterlife.

At the reception following,
my wife and I watched a mob of disciples
rush up to him,
young men and women
in their thirties,
thrilled to be in the presence
of the great man.

Charismatic and as charming
as he'd always been on television,
the Famous Atheist
cracked jokes
about the end of the world,
compared god to Kim Jong Il,
made people laugh,
while reminding them
how religion still poisoned
everything.

As more and more followers
descended on him,
asking for autographs,
pressing copies of his best-selling
book into his famous hands,
telling unsolicited tales of their own
conversion,
giving praise to the man
who had saved them,

the Famous Atheist,
growing tired of their worshiping
his every gesture,
unintentionally
threw up his hands,
and they all bowed.

What If We Just Stopped Calling Death *Death?*

What if we refused to call death anything
or even to acknowledge it exists?
Like some ex-lover-turned-stalker you run into at the bar,
you pretend you've never met before,
not wanting to give her the satisfaction
of knowing her name,
or worse some pet name you shared,
that always made her seem much nicer
and softer than she really was.

Maybe Death will feel the same.
Maybe Death will be so busy courting some other sucker,
someone you think you recognize,
someone you'd warn if you weren't so selfishly
trying to go unnoticed,
that she won't even see you there,
standing dignified by the bar,
stubborn in your refusal to budge,
despite knowing eventually everyone relents.

What if there were a restraining order
you could take out against Death?
One or two glances from those crazy eyes
reminding you of all the unresolved grievances
last time you had a brush,
making you long for protection,
making you realize it might be better if you left,
found a hideout in some livelier place,
one you're certain she's never been,

all the while checking over your shoulder,
growing confident with every step
that you've finally cheated Death,
just to find her waiting by the bar for you,
your last sobering drink already on her tab,
as someone slips past
you think you recognize,
looking the other way.

Marc Chagall: *The Juggler*, 1943

Christ the clown.
Muhammad the acrobat.
Buddha the lion tamer.

The circus is religion.
The circus is human.
The circus is bird?

Juggler of time.
Fiddler of the universe.
A girl rides by on a miniature horse.

Blue as Earth.
Red as rooster.
Hold the clock upside down.

Learn to juggle
by mastering one object first.
Never juggle what can't be dropped.

Never juggle women
or friends or children
or health.

Juggle words,
but when necessary
learn to toss.

No one is impressed
how long you hold them—
this circus is short.

Go ride a unicycle.

Time Line

> "In today's world," said John Britton, an AT&T spokesman, "there are just too many other ways to get this information. You can look at your cellphone or your computer. You no longer have to pick up the telephone."

Like a sweet old grandma, you were there for me.
I could call day or night and hear your voice.
It didn't matter if you were automated,
or recorded long ago, you always answered
and never screened your calls.
"At the tone the time will be," you'd say.
I took that expression with me everywhere as a kid
and used it whenever anybody asked.
I wondered if they had a version of you in France,
in which you said, À la tone, l'heure sera...
You, who were always waiting.
When was your last transmission?
Who was the last desperate caller?
Where would we have been without you?
Late for every appointment,
missing every bus and plane,
forgetting people's weddings.
Was it better before clocks and sundials?
Before computers and cellphones?
Before we needed you at all?
When we tracked our days by celestial movements,
births and deaths by flood and earthquake
age by lines across a person's face?
  "Hand me the phone," my father would say,
whenever he wanted to set his watch,
long before his own plug got pulled
and there wasn't any number
I could dial to reach him.
Long before I ever dreamed
that time could end.

I Don't Believe in Ghosts

And if I ever were to see one,
I couldn't say I'd find it very comforting,
or even believe what I saw.

My sister gets disappointed
my father hasn't contacted her yet,
as if it were a prerequisite of the dead.

I suppose I'd feel resentful too,
kind of like when you call someone
and they don't call you back.

Which is one reason
I've never believed in an afterlife—
I know how to take a hint.

Looking in People's Houses

My wife thinks it's creepy of me, & I admit,
she's probably right. Still, it doesn't stop me
when we take our nightly walks around the neighborhood.
It's not that I'm out to compare anything
or hope to catch a glimpse of

some good-looking woman in a towel crossing her hallway
(which would be perverted after all),
& I don't do it in the way my mom used to make my dad

drive around rich neighborhoods,
as some masochistic maneuver to make
themselves feel inadequate.

"It's just creepy," says my wife.

But I can't help myself.
I want to see how people spend their nights.
How they sit in their family rooms. What they hang on
their walls. I want to see the different body language
between different husbands & different wives—
do they sit close together,
or are they like my parents who fell asleep
on separate couches watching television
every night? I want to see what people eat for dinner.
Are they drinking wine? Screaming at each other?
Picking their nose? What are they thinking about?
Are they anxious? Sick? Tired? Hopeless?

"Look," says my wife, tugging on my arm
& trying to lure my attention
from one of the houses,
"you can see a lot of stars tonight."

But tonight I'm less interested
in my neighbors trillions of miles away
than I am those much closer to me,
who tell me all I need to know
about the universe.

The Math Mortician

Instead of bodies, he sees numbers,
readies them up on time's table,
dresses them in brackets,

uses algorithms over aspirate
to extract each variable,
hypothesizes infinity is but an empty set,

and life an interval between two ends,
whose value isn't absolute,
when death's the only constant.

The New York Quarterly Foundation, Inc.
New York, New York

Poetry Magazine

Since 1969

Edgy, fresh, groundbreaking, eclectic—voices from all walks of life.

Definitely NOT your mama's poetry magazine!

The *New York Quarterly* has been defining the term contemporary American poetry since its first craft interview with W. H. Auden.

Interviews • Essays • and of course, lots of poems.

www.nyquarterly.org

No contest! That's correct, NYQ Books are NO CONTEST to other small presses because we do not support ourselves through contests. Our books are carefully selected by invitation only, so you know that NYQ Books are produced with the same editorial integrity as the magazine that has brought you the most eclectic contemporary American poetry since 1969.

Books

nyqbooks.org

poetry at the edge™

www.ingramcontent.com/pod-product-compliance
Lightning Source LLC
LaVergne TN
LVHW041343080426
835512LV00006B/589